DISASTER ALERT!

Flood and Monsoon Alert!

Rachel Eagen

Crabtree Publishing Company
www.crabtreebooks.com

presented by:

Crabtree Publishing Company
www.crabtreebooks.com

This book is for Lindsay McNiff

Coordinating editor: Ellen Rodger

Project editor: Sean Charlebois

Book design and production coordinator: Rosie Gowsell

Cover design: Rob MacGregor

Photo research: Allison Napier

Copyediting and indexing: Adrianna Morganelli

Scanning technician: Arlene Arch-Wilson

Consultant: Professor John Pomeroy, Canada Research Chair in Water Resources and Climate Change, Centre for Hydrology, Department of Geography, University of Saskatchewan

Photographs: AP/ Wide World Photos: p. 6, p. 15 (bottom), p. 20, p. 29 (top); Dave Bartruff/ CORBIS/ MAGMA: p. 3; Tom Bean Photography: p. 28; Bettman/ CORBIS/ MAGMA: p. 13; CORBIS/ MAGMA: p. 9; Peter Crabtree: p. 16; Bob Daemmrich/ CORBIS/ MAGMA: p. 26; Warren Faidley/ Weatherstock: p. 21; Fema News Photo: p. 4, p. 14, p. 24, p. 27 (top); Owen Franken/ CORBIS/ MAGMA: p. 22 (bottom); Cape Grim B.A.P.S./ Simon Fraser/SCIENCE PHOTO LIBRARY: p. 19; Robert Holmes/ CORBIS: p. 27 (bottom); Rich Iwasaki/ Getty Images: p. 1; Jacques Jangoux/ Photo Researchers, Inc: p. 7; The Jewish Museum, NY/ Art Resource, NY: p. 17 (top); Wolfgang Kaehler: p. 11, p. 25;

Keith Kent / SCIENCE PHOTO LIBRARY: p. 17 (bottom); Paolo Koch/ Photo Researchers, Inc: p. 8; Vittoriano Rastelli/ CORBIS/ MAGMA: p. 15 (top); Dean Sewell/ Panos Pictures: p. 23 (bottom); Ben Spencer; Eye Ubiquitous/ CORBIS/ MAGMA: p. 5 (top); Frank Staub /Index Stock Imagery: p. 18; Paul Taylor/ Index Stock Imagery: p. 29 (bottom); Adam Woolfitt/ CORBIS/ MAGMA: p. 5 (bottom); Michael S. Yamashita/ CORBIS/ MAGMA: p. 22 (top), p. 23 (top).

Illustrations: Dan Pressman: p. 7, p. 9, pp. 10-11, pp. 12-13; David Wysotski, Allure Illustrations: pp. 30-31

Cover: Floods endanger the lives of people and animals caught unaware.

Contents: Flash floods can happen nearly everywhere on Earth. On the flat land in arid climates, a sudden rainfall can cause flash floods that sweep cars off the road and carry them great distances.

Title page: Cars sit submersed in water from a flood.

Crabtree Publishing Company
www.crabtreebooks.com   1-800-387-7650

Cataloging-in-Publication data

Eagen, Rachel, 1979-
    Flood and monsoon alert! / written by Rachel Eagen.
        p. cm. -- (Disaster alert!)
    Includes index.
    ISBN 0-7787-1577-9 (rlb) -- ISBN 0-7787-1609-0 (pbk)
    1. Floods--Juvenile literature. 2. Monsoons--Juvenile literature.
I. Title. II. Series.
    GB1399.E29 2004
    551.48'9--dc22
                                                    2004013053
                                                        LC

**Published in
the United States**
PMB 16A
350 Fifth Ave.
Suite 3308
New York, NY
10118

**Published
in Canada**
616 Welland Ave.
St. Catharines
Ontario, Canada
L2M 5V6

**Published in the
United Kingdom**
73 Lime Walk
Headington
Oxford
0X3 7AD
United Kingdom

**Published
in Australia**
386 Mt. Alexander Rd.
Ascot Vale (Melbourne)
V1C 3032

Table of Contents

Water Gone Wild

Floods can happen any time, anywhere, and are the most destructive natural disasters on Earth. Floods are caused by rainfall, burst dams, choked river channels, snow melt, and sudden, violent thunderstorms. In some parts of the world, floods are a common side effect of the summer monsoon.

Floods wipe out entire communities and cause millions of dollars worth of damage. Recently, scientists have been able to predict where and when floods will occur, but communities can never fully prevent the devastating effects of a flood.

(above) Flooding rivers destroyed hundreds of homes and businesses in the Midwest United States in the summer of 1994.

What is a disaster? A disaster is a destructive event that affects the natural world and human communities. Some disasters are predictable and others occur without warning. Coping successfully with a disaster depends on a community's preparation.

Seasonal floods

A monsoon is an **air mass** that stretches for several thousand miles over India and Southeast Asia. The air mass blows in one direction during the winter, and shifts to blow in the opposite direction in the summer. The summer and winter monsoons bring two very different types of weather. The summer monsoon brings heavy storms. Monsoonal rains are hazardous when they fall for too long, causing rivers to burst their **banks** and flood the land.

(right) People are caught in the steamy summer monsoon rain in Simla, India. The term "monsoon" comes from the Arabic word mausim, *meaning "seasons."*

Storm serpent

According to ancient Chinese legends, water gods known as dragons controlled the rains. Dragons who lived in palaces deep beneath the sea decided when the rains would fall and how much water they would bring. When the dragon was angry he sent rains and caused a flood. As a way of honoring the water god and warding off disaster, the people of China began the traditions of dragon boat racing and dragon dancing. The dragon boat race was held on the first day of summer. The Chinese people thought honoring dragons protected the harvest from floods. The dragon dance imitates the movement of water in a tidal wave. Legendary dragon sightings were a sign of future happiness or wealth.

Science of Floods

A flood occurs when the level of water in a river rises, either quickly or over time, and spills over its banks and covers the surrounding area. This area is called the floodplain.

River systems

A river is a large natural stream of water that empties into a bigger body of water, such as an ocean. Rivers are fed by smaller streams and creeks called tributaries. Rain that falls in the area around a river and its tributaries, called the river basin, can either run off into the tributaries, or be absorbed by the soil. As long as the ground is very dry, the **porous** soil absorbs the excess water. Water is drawn downward through the soil through a natural process called infiltration. Once water reaches the water table, which is a reservoir of water beneath the Earth's surface, it cannot seep down any further. When the soil is already full of water, or saturated, the water cannot be absorbed and it pools on top of the land like a shallow lake.

Soil erosion

Soil **erosion** is partly caused by floods. Bodies of water move according to **currents**. Flowing water is strong enough to transport objects as small as grains of sand or as large as tree trunks. Soil along the banks and riverbeds is moved from one place to another by flowing water. As soil is deposited and builds up along a stretch of riverbed, the river becomes shallower, and there is less room for the water to flow. Slow-moving rivers are more likely to flood because they deposit much more **sediment** along the riverbanks and riverbed, slowly raising them above the floodplain.

(above) As flood waters rise, people and animals are forced to seek higher ground.

Meandering rivers

The course of a river changes over time and creates a floodplain. As the water flows in a stream, it slowly erodes the bank on one side, transporting the soil to the other side, further downstream. This creates strong, high banks on one side and weaker, eroded banks on the other. Eventually, the river's path widens, and a vast floodplain is made.

The floodplain of the lower Amazon River in South America is seen here at a low water level. When the river floods, the islands in the middle and green jungle on both sides will be completely covered in water.

Water cycle

The water cycle keeps water moving around the Earth. The sun's rays heat water over oceans and cause the water to evaporate, or change into a gas, called vapor. When the vapor rises into the cooler air above, it condenses into water droplets and forms clouds. When clouds cannot hold any more moisture, the moisture falls to the Earth as rain or snow. This is known as precipitation. Precipitation is absorbed by the soil and seeps down to the water table, or runs off over the land and flows back into the ocean.

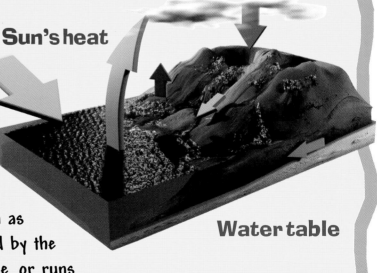

Evaporating water (vapor) **Precipitation**

Sun's heat

Water table

Monsoon in the Making

A monsoon is an enormous air mass that blows in one direction during the winter, making the land hot and dry, then shifts to blow in the opposite direction during the summer, bringing heavy rains. The monsoon current is a constant cycle that is powered by the sun, air currents, air pressure, and the Coriolis Effect.

A street during heavy monsoon rain in Benares, India. People in monsoon climates have learned to cope with the seasonal rains.

Heat engine

The sun shines on various parts of the Earth at different times, which is why we experience both day and night. This is due to the rotation of the Earth. The tilt of the Earth's **axis** also affects what parts of the Earth are exposed to the sun. This gives us our seasons. Around the month of May, the sun shines to the north of the **equator**, directly onto the countries bordering the Indian Ocean and the China Sea, including India, Thailand, Bangladesh, and Myanmar. As the sun shines, the land becomes much warmer than the ocean. The air over the land becomes lighter as it heats up and begins to rise. When this happens, cool, moisture-laden sea winds rush toward the continent to replace the rising warm air.

Air currents

An air current is a vast mass of air that moves in one continuous motion. The winds that blow just north and south of the equator are called the trade winds. As the dry, warm continental air rises in the summer, cool sea air blows toward the continent from a southwest direction. These winds are called the Southwestern Trade Winds.

Air pressure

Air pressure also helps to drive the monsoon current. Air flows from an area of high pressure to an area of lower pressure. A region of low air pressure develops over the land as it heats up. Higher air pressure over the sea naturally moves into the land as hot land air rises. Low air pressure is known for heavy storms. Low air pressure and the inland movement of the Southwestern Trade Winds create the perfect conditions for monsoonal rains in the summer.

The Coriolis Effect

The spinning of the Earth affects the movement of the trade winds, because the Earth rotates at a higher speed than the winds. The trade winds originating in the south should move north in a straight line toward the equator. Likewise, the trade winds coming from the north should move south in a straight line toward the equator. Instead, the trade winds are bent until they run almost parallel to the equator. This happens because of the force exerted by Earth's spin. The curving action of the winds is called the Coriolis Effect. Gravity enhances the Coriolis Effect by pulling the air down toward the center of the Earth.

Northeasterly Trade winds

Southwesterly Trade winds

(above) Air currents are constantly on the move all over the globe. These winds are named according to where they occur and the direction in which they flow.

(below) A view of monsoons over the Brahmaputra River, and nearby floodplains in East India and Bangladesh.

Life of a Flood

A flood begins when water in a river rises until it spills over the river's banks and rushes over the nearby floodplain. A river's water level can rise because of heavy rainfall, melting snow, and choked river channels.

Rainfall

When rain washes down mountains it sometimes causes flooding in the valley below. Rain also causes flooding by adding water to rivers with naturally high water levels. Even a slow-moving rainstorm can cause flooding, since the rain falls in one area for a long period of time.

Choked channels

Ice and debris, such as tree leaves, can block a river and prevent it from flowing along its natural course. Flooding is likely when this happens, because there is nowhere for the water to go, so it pours onto the floodplain.

Melting snow

Snow high in the mountains begins to melt in spring. As temperatures rise, snow turns to water, and flows down the mountainside. Strong sunshine or spring rain also helps snow to melt. The land cannot usually absorb both the melt water and spring showers combined, so it is common for flooding to occur in communities located at the base of mountains.

Flood crest

The highest elevation of the water level during a flood is called the crest. Once a flood crests, the water begins to recede slowly as it seeps into the ground or evaporates.

Flash floods

A flash flood is a flood that occurs without warning. Flash floods are caused by sudden, violent thunderstorms during which the rain falls too quickly to be absorbed by the land. Trickling streams turn into raging rivers and overflow onto the saturated floodplain. Flash floods cause cars to skid off roads, and sweep away people and buildings in low-lying areas.

(above) Flash floods happen with such incredible speed that some people do not have time to get to higher ground.

Life of a Monsoon

A monsoon is a continuous cycle of air that changes direction twice a year. When the winds blow from the southwest, they generally cause wet weather, and when they blow from the northeast, they cause dry, and sometimes cold weather.

Summer/Southwest Monsoon

The southwest monsoon happens during the summer and affects India, Bangladesh, and Southeast Asia. Other areas that are affected by summer monsoonal rains are Japan and China.

Winter/Northeast Monsoon

By the end of September, the rains slow down as the Northeasterly Trade Winds blow out to sea from the Asian continent. These cool, dry winds bring mild weather to India and China.

Summer Monsoon

1. Beginning around May, the Southwesterly Trade Winds cross the Bay of Bengal, and pick up moisture from the sea (blue arrows). These winds increase in speed and eventually reach the east coast of India. They bring storms that are blown northward across the country.

2. At the same time, swirling masses of air form over the Arabian Sea and travel to the west coast of India, delivering storms that meet with the rains from the east coast. With both storm systems crossing the country at once, India receives a thorough soaking between May and September.

(right) Cherrapunji, India, experiences so much rainfall that it has been named "the wettest place on earth." One summer monsoon brought 902 inches (2,290 cm) of rain! Flooding is less common in Cherrapunji because it is located 4,232 feet (1,290 meters) above sea level.

Winter Monsoon

1. Once the northeasterly trade winds cross the Bay of Bengal, in India, they are warmed by rising moisture from the sea. This helps to deliver rain to Indonesia and Australia. Meanwhile, freezing cold winds are blown southward from Siberia, bringing streams of cold air across India.

2. India remains dry at this time of year, but dust storms are common in China. Due to their southern location in the Indian Ocean, places such as Sumatra, Borneo, and Indonesia are soaked by both the southwest and northeast monsoon.

Famous Floods

Floods from rivers and monsoons have caused some of the world's worst disasters. In the United States, floods have taken more human lives than any other natural disaster. Entire cities have had to be rebuilt because of the ravages of floods.

Despite the dangers of flooding, millions of people live in the area around the Mississippi River in the Midwest of the United States. Excessive rainfall in the summer of 1994 led to floods which destroyed many homes and businesses.

Yellow River, China

The Yellow River has been called "China's Sorrow" because it has killed more people than any other river in the world. The Yellow River begins high in the northern mountains of China and travels 3,000 miles (4,828 km) to the Yellow Sea. The riverbed of the Yellow River has been raised through years of soil **deposition**, a process in which millions of tons of yellow mud settled on the Yellow River's bed. This has made the riverbed higher than the surrounding countryside in places, and has led to terrible flooding. One of the worst floods occurred during the summer monsoon rains of 1931. Nearly four million people drowned and many villages within the floodplain were completely wiped out. Many other people died from outbreaks of waterborne diseases, such as **typhoid** and **cholera**.

Bangladesh

Monsoon flooding occurs regularly in Bangladesh, a small country near India. In 1988, the summer monsoon arrived earlier than usual, and the people were not prepared. When the rivers overflowed, flooding killed approximately 1,600 people and left 25 million without homes. Businesses and storefronts in cities were washed away. In the countryside, the floodwaters ripped young rice plants from the ground and destroyed vast amounts of cropland which led to famine.

(right) A cyclist wades through a street in Florence, Italy, in 1966. The flooding of the Arno River caused damage to the city's vast collections of art, sculpture, and books.

(below) Residents of Bangladesh carry clean drinking water as they wade through floodwaters in 1998. Three weeks of rain during the summer monsoon caused the Ganges, Brahmaputra, and Meghna Rivers to spill over their banks. Ten million people were left homeless.

Red River, Canada

The city of Winnipeg, Canada, was built on the banks of the Red River, which floods from time to time. In 1950, the citizens of Winnipeg and the surrounding area prepared for the worst flood yet. An especially harsh winter left huge snow deposits, and April thunderstorms combined with melting snow caused the river to swell. Dikes, or flood barriers, were softened by the **inundation** and eventually collapsed, leaving the city defenseless. People from many communities were forced to evacuate, or leave their homes, and thousands of cattle either drowned or were shot by farmers who had lost the cropland needed to feed them.

For thousands of years, the Nile River in Egypt flooded every summer. The ancient Egyptians called this the "Gift of the Nile" because the fertile mud that the flood spread over the soil helped crops grow.
In the 1960s, the Egyptian government built the Aswan High Dam to flood an even larger part of the Nile Valley. Many ancient monuments, such as the temple of Abu Simbel, had to be taken apart and moved to safety.

Mississippi and Missouri Rivers, U.S.A.

In 1993, a series of warm air currents originating in the Gulf of Mexico produced about 200 serious thunderstorms from June to August in the Midwest United States. This weather **phenomenon**, which occurs about every seven years, is known as **El Niño**. The large amount of rainfall brought by these storms caused the massive Missouri and Mississippi rivers to flood. Millions of dollars of damage to crops occurred and 45,000 homes were destroyed. Many people drowned in the floodwaters, while several thousand were evacuated from their communities. Volunteers came from around the world to provide relief to the victims.

Lynmouth, England

The seaside village of Lynmouth, England, sits 1,500 feet (457 meters) below a forested cliff, in a Y-shaped valley where two rivers, the East and West Lyn, meet. On August 15, 1952, torrential downpours caused the East and West Lyns to surge. Rain falling onto the neighboring cliff raged downhill to inundate the village. Water gushed down in a flash flood, dislodging heavy boulders that had destroyed and buried the village by morning.

(right) Flood stories have been told by many ancient peoples. One of the most famous stories is about Noah, who built a boat called an ark and took two of every animal on board during a flood that lasted 40 days and 40 nights.

Arizona Monsoon

The United States experiences a small-scale monsoon season. Each spring, winter winds blowing from the northwest shift to blow from the southeast. These southeasterly winds pick up moisture from the Gulf of Mexico. Thunderstorms in Arizona are common from June to September, but the rains are not continuous like they are in India during this time.

Warning Signs

In ancient times, scientists relied upon the position of the stars and planets to predict the weather. Today, meteorologists, or scientists who study the weather, use scientific instruments to determine where and when floods are likely to occur months in advance. With proper warning, communities can protect themselves and their homes from flooding.

Forecasting floods

Scientists can predict the chance of a flood by collecting information on specific rivers. A scientist observes a river's hydrology, or the way the land causes a river to flow. By measuring the size of the river basin, scientists can tell how much extra water a river can hold from precipitation before it overflows its banks. Meteorologists then calculate how much rain falls in a particular area on average. Next, hydrologists, or scientists who study water, determine how much of the annual precipitation actually ends up in the river. This depends upon the surrounding landscape, and whether or not the river or lake is easily accessed by **runoff**. Finally, hydrologists calculate how much water can be expected to flow into the river by adding up all of these factors.

Flood gauges are used around the world to measure the crest of floods. Each segment on the gauge measures one foot (0.3 meters) and as a river's floodwaters rise, scientists can tell how large of an area will be flooded.

Watches and warnings

The National Weather Service is a network of thirteen forecast centers in the United States that collect weather data and issue severe weather warnings, such as flood watches and warnings. Meteorologists measure precipitation amounts against the height of rivers to forecast whether or not a flood is likely. Flood warnings can be issued months before they occur, allowing people time to protect their homes from water damage. Proper preparation before a flood is essential in lessening recovery time and effort.

Forecasting monsoons

The monsoon forecast has been called the world's most important weather prediction, because half of the world's population would starve if the rains did not come. Months before the summer monsoon, meteorologists try to pinpoint exactly when the rains will arrive. Scientists gather information on temperature, air pressure, and snow cover. High temperatures and low air pressure help to bring the rains. Melting snow in the mountains not only indicates that the land is heating rapidly, but that it is evaporating into the sky to add moisture to the clouds.

(top) Scientists collect information about rivers at gauging stations. Inside each station, instruments such as a float-tape gauge measure the changing water level of a river.

(left) By sending out radio waves that reflect off water droplets or ice particles, and measuring the returning waves, Doppler radar determines whether a storm is coming closer or moving away.

19

Path of a Flood

Most floods occur in natural areas, when a river overflows its banks and spills onto its floodplain. The water is dispersed on the floodplain and the river is said to be in spate, or in flood. Most rivers spill into the floodplain once every two years. Floods can also occur from burst dams, glaciers, and storms.

Burst dams

Dams are built to control rivers that frequently flood. The pressure of the water behind a dam can produce tiny cracks in the concrete wall. When left unattended, these cracks grow and spread, making the dam frail. As water pressure builds on one side, the dam becomes less capable of supporting it, allowing small leaks to trickle through. These leaks can quickly cause the dam to crumble. When dams burst, terrible floods result. Bursting can be prevented as long as cracks and leaks, no matter how small, are fixed properly and immediately. Dams also burst during earthquakes, rock falls, or mudslides that occur where the dam is built.

(above) When the South Fork Dam collapsed in 1889, water flooded Johnstown, Pennsylvania, and killed more than 2,000 people.

Glacier lake bursts

Glaciers are slow-moving, frozen rivers that are formed from the build-up of snow and ice over many years. Glaciers are so big that they can dam the flow of water in rivers. When a glacier melts, it adds large quantities of water into oceans and rivers. When this happens suddenly, it is called a glacier lake burst. The added amount of water from a glacier lake burst can cause rivers to swell and surge, and bring on a flood.

Storm surge

Hurricanes and other ocean storms bring ocean waters to shore in sudden, destructive waves called storm surges. In the open ocean, these waves can be up to fifteen feet (4.5 meters) above sea level. The surge forms over the ocean within a low-pressure zone called the eye of the storm. The low pressure sucks ocean waters upward, forming a bulge that is less noticeable out at sea. As the hurricane travels inland, the storm surge grows in height and then crashes over coastal villages causing flooding.

Seiche

A seiche occurs on lakefronts when high winds cause the water to slosh from side to side. Eventually, the water builds up so much momentum that the water spills over the lip of the basin in a sudden swell. Seiches cause damage to homes built close to the shore.

Washouts

When water saturates the ground below a building or road, the soil that makes up its foundation can erode and fall away. This is called a washout. Washouts are common during seiches and flash floods. In the photos below, the soil under a house is quickly worn away by the flood waters.

Path of a Monsoon

A monsoon brings many kinds of weather to different parts of the world. Monsoons can bring intense rains that last for months and cause floods in one part of the world, while causing dust storms, bush fires, and droughts in others.

Monsoons are a necessary part of life in India, China, and Southeast Asia. Without the rainy season, the rice crop would fail and half the population would starve. The Chinese call the rains, meiyu, or plum rains, because they allow fruit to ripen on the trees.

Summer monsoon

The summer monsoon brings much-needed relief to the hot, dry lands of India and Southeast Asia. The people of India celebrate the summer monsoon with a festival called Teej. A colorful parade of decorated elephants, camels, and horses walk through the streets, while families dressed in vibrant clothing gather to watch. Women sing songs to welcome the fruitful rains. During the summer monsoon, rice paddies are nourished. At the end of the monsoon, farmers venture out into their fields to harvest the rice. In Australia, the summer monsoon brings a dry season, not rain. In the southern part of the country, terrible droughts can occur at this time.

(right) Banana leaves are used as umbrellas in parts of the world where monsoons are a part of daily life.

Winter monsoon

The winter monsoon brings dry, mild weather to the places that were soaked by the summer monsoon rains. India becomes dry and it hardly rains again there from October until the following May. Parts of China turn very cold, as freezing winds blow south from Siberia, kicking up dust and sand to create storms that make seeing and breathing difficult. Meanwhile, Australia receives heavy rains, especially along the northern coast. Sometimes the rains are so intense that flooding causes power failures and prevents cars from traveling on the roads.

(above) During the winter monsoon in China, called gudjeng, *the northern parts of the country turn very cold, and winds whip up dust and sand.*

The winter monsoon rains in Australia make the vegetation very lush. When the summer monsoon comes, the lush vegetation is dried up by the hot winds that blow over the land. This makes it easy for wildfires to start. Wildfires spread quickly in Australia and are fueled by dry grasses and shrubs.

When a Flood Strikes

Monsoons are predictable storms. People living in monsoon climates expect the rains to come at a particular time, so they are usually prepared when they happen. Unlike monsoons, floods can occur anywhere in the world, so it is important to know what to do if a flood strikes.

Preparing for the worst

When a flood threatens a community, there is usually enough time to prepare. People work together to build temporary barriers called dikes, built out of sandbags to protect homes, businesses, and farmland. All power should be turned off to prevent floodwaters from becoming charged with electricity and electrocuting relief workers. Local relief organizations, such as the **Red Cross** or **Red Crescent** can supply information on emergency procedures, a community's flood evacuation plan, and where to seek shelter if people have to leave their homes.

Sandbags are used to build temporary barriers to prevent flood waters from spreading. Home damage can be prevented with the construction of sandbag barriers. Sandbags should be filled halfway, and then piled around the foundation of a house. The sand will prevent the water from seeping through tiny cracks in the foundation of the house, or from breaking through ground-floor windows.

Flood supplies kit

Any supplies a family might need to survive if the power is cut off or evacuation occurs during a flood should be kept together, including:

* First aid kit
* Blankets
* Bottled water
* Extra clothing and shoes
* Non-perishable food
* Can opener

* Flashlight
* Batteries
* Rain gear
* Map of the area

Plan an escape route

Every family should decide where to go in the event of an evacuation. It is a good idea to have a family contact, such as a friend or a relative. It is important that this person lives out of the area, because that person is less likely to experience flooding at the same time. Decide who this person will be, write down his/her phone number, and keep a copy of it by the phone, on the fridge, and in the family flood supplies kit.

Safety during flash floods

There is rarely any warning before a flash flood, so it is important to act quickly. Get out of the way of the floodwaters, since they move very fast and are strong enough to sweep people off of their feet and cars off of the road. Some people have saved their lives by climbing trees. Other safe areas might be the second floor of a house, an attic, or even a roof if it can be reached safely. Roadblocks should be obeyed as they warn of dangerous areas, such as bridges.

If you are in a car that will not start, get out immediately and move to higher ground. Never try to swim or walk in floodwaters.

Receding Water

Floods and monsoons cause irreparable damage to homes, cities, and the environment. Once the water level lowers, or recedes, cleaning up is extremely costly. Government assistance and the work of volunteers help communities recover.

After a flood

Floodwaters cause enormous damage. The water is contaminated by raw sewage and dangerous floating debris, such as nails and broken glass. Fallen power lines can charge floodwaters, electrocuting anyone who tries to walk in them. Food and water that come into contact with floodwaters becomes **contaminated**, so emergency crews advise everyone to boil their water for at least five minutes to make it safe to use. Roads and damaged bridges have to be repaired, so it is common for communities to remain evacuated while cleanup operations are underway. Farmers need to replant destroyed crops in fields that have not been too heavily damaged by sand.

(above) Residents clean up in Texas after the Guadalupe River flooded. Flood victims should never return to their homes until authorities say it is safe to do so.

Permanent barriers

The construction of permanent barriers helps protect communities from future floods. Dams and levees are made of high cement walls that keep floodwaters at bay. Dams contain huge reservoirs of water which help to generate electricity, supply drinking water, and **irrigate** cropland. Dams are expensive, large-scale construction projects. There are hundreds of thousands of dams in use today all over the world, all working to hold back major rivers and to channel excess water out to sea. A spillway is a structure that is built close to the dam and is used to channel water downstream. The spillway prevents water from spilling over the dam walls by maintaining a constant water level.

(above) Relief efforts come from the combined help of governments, emergency crews, and volunteers. These people work to repair damaged homes, and provide food, medical attention, and temporary shelter to flood victims.

A levee is a permanent barrier constructed to prevent floodwaters from reaching communities. This levee in Rivertown, Mississippi is made from concrete and stretches many miles along the banks of the Mississippi River.

Floodways

Floodways are strips of land along a river that are left bare. Homes are not built in floodways, so that if a flood occurs, the water cannot cause damage to buildings in the low-lying floodplain. A floodway looks like a bare valley, and sometimes a structure such as a road or railroad track is built to cross from one side to the other.

Floodwalls

In some cities, the banks of a river are replaced by huge concrete barriers called floodwalls. These walls are built to prevent the waters of a river from spilling into the city.

(right) Water shoots into a spillway at Glen Canyon Dam on the Colorado River.

Control at Three Gorges

The Three Gorges Dam Project is an expensive flood control project in China. The Chinese government debated the project for nearly 40 years, and finally approved construction in 1942. When finished, the dam will be 594 feet (181 meters) high and will create huge quantities of electricity. The resulting reservoir will be 412 miles (663 km) long and will flood many hundreds of Chinese villages along the Yellow River. As many as one million people will need to move because their villages will be flooded by the reservoir.

Dikes

A dike is a long wall or embankment built at the edge of a river or lake to protect the land against flooding when the water surges. Dikes can be made from almost any material, but their durability depends upon the strength of materials used for construction. Permanent dikes are made from steel and concrete. Temporary dikes are built when there is little warning before a flood occurs. Sandbags are commonly used to construct temporary dikes. Other barrier materials include sediment dikes, which are sturdy bags that can be filled with water and sediment.

Learning to adapt

Most communities that experience a monsoon season have adapted to the flooding of rivers. The rainy season is relied upon in monsoonal climates for healthy crops to feed the population. In China and India, farmers build low mud walls to trap the monsoonal rains that help the rice crop flourish.

(above) A flood dike erected by residents and volunteers in Drayton, North Dakota, keeps Red River floodwaters from entering the town in April 1997.

The city of New Orleans, Louisiana, is built below sea level. A complex system of flood prevention machinery, including floodgate and pumps, is used to make sure the water of the Mississippi River and the Gulf of Mexico stay at a constant level and do not flood the city. Pumping stations keep the water at the right levels.

Recipe for Disaster

Here is a simple activity to make your own barometer that will help you understand air pressure and its effect on weather.

What you need:

*A straight-sided glass or beaker
*A twelve inch (30 cm) ruler
*Tape
*One foot (30 cm) of clear plastic tubing
*Chewing gum
*Black marker
*Water

What to do:

1. Stand the ruler inside the glass or beaker and tape it against the side.

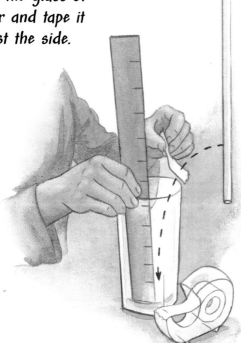

2. Place the tubing next to the ruler in an upright position. Tape it one inch (2.5 cm) from the bottom of the glass.

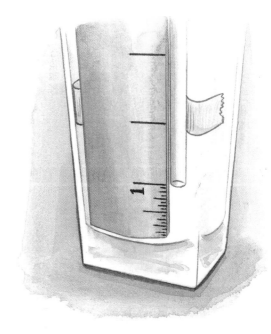

3. Chew a piece of gum until it is soft. Fill the glass halfway with water. Suck on the tube like a straw to draw up some of the water, then quickly place the gum over the top of the tube to trap it.

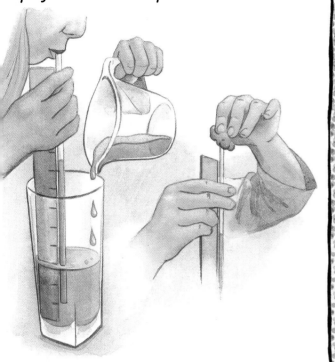

4. Use the marker to indicate the water level. Observe the water level over several days and continue to make marks to show the rising and falling of the water level.

What you will see:

As the air pressure increases, it pushes down on the water in the glass and forces some of it up the tube. This indicates clear weather. As the air pressure decreases, it allows the trapped water to travel back down the tube and into the glass. Low air pressure indicates stormy weather.

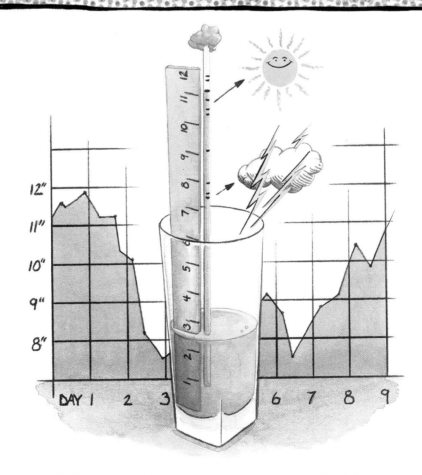

Glossary

air mass A large volume of air that is the same in temperature and humidity

air pressure The measure of how close or far apart air particles are in an air mass

axis A straight line on which an object turns. The Earth's axis passes through the North and South Poles

bank The sloping land along the edge of a river or lake

barometer An instrument that measures the pressure of the atmosphere. A barometer is used to forecast the weather

cholera A serious disease caused by bacteria that affects the small intestine

contaminate To pollute

current The path or flow of air or water in motion

deposition The laying down of matter through a natural process

drought A period of little or no rain

El Niño A warm ocean current that travels to South America

equator The imaginary line around the middle of the Earth

erosion The process of being worn away, as by water and wind

inundation The overflow of floodwaters

irrigate To supply land with water

phenomenon An event that can be observed

porous Containing tiny holes

Red Cross/Red Crescent An international organization that cares for people who are sick, wounded, or left homeless by wars or natural disasters

runoff Water that drains or flows off the surface of the land

sediment Small rock fragments such as sand, clay, and gravel that settle in layers on land or on the ocean floor

tidal wave A rise in water along a shore caused by a storm

typhoid A contagious disease that is caused by bacteria in dirty food or water

Index

1 2 3 4 5 6 7 8 9 0 Printed in the U.S.A. 3 2 1 0 9 8 7 6 5 4